waiting

waiting

—

A Time to Hear
God's Voice

FRED CLOUD

UPPER
ROOM BOOKS®
NASHVILLE

The Upper Room® Web site: www.upperroom.org

UPPER ROOM®, UPPER ROOM BOOKS®, and design logos are
trademarks owned by The Upper Room®, a ministry of GBOD®,
Nashville, Tennessee. All rights reserved.

Unless otherwise noted, scripture quotations are from the New
Revised Standard Version Bible, copyright 1989 Division of Christian
Education of the National Council of the Churches of Christ in the
United States of America. Used by permission. All rights reserved.

Scripture noted RSV is from the Revised Standard Version of the Bible,
copyright 1952 (2nd edition, 1971) by the Division of Christian Education of the National Council of the Churches of Christ in the United
States of America. Used by permission. All rights reserved.

Excerpt from *A Day of Rest: Creating a Spiritual Space in Your Week* by
Martha Whitmore Hickman, copyright © 1999 by Martha Whitmore
Hickman. Used by permission of Abingdon Press.

Excerpt from "Fall from Grace: How Modern Life Has Made Waiting
a Desperate Act," by Noelle Oxenhandler, originally published in *The
New Yorker*, June 16, 1997, used by permission of the author.

Cover and interior design: Bruce Gore / www.gorestudio.com
Cover image: Photonica / Getty Images; photo by Wataru Yanagida
Typesetting: PerfecType, Nashville, TN
First printing: 2009

LIBRARY OF CONGRESS CATALOGING-IN-PUBLICATION DATA
Cloud, Fred
    Waiting : a time to hear God's voice / Fred Cloud.
        p. cm.
ISBN 978-0-8358-9993-2
1. Prayers. I. Title.
BV260.C63 2009
242—dc22   2009027230

Dedicated with unending love and gratitude

for the lives of my wife,

Barbara Dickerson Cloud;

my daughter, Amanda Karen Cloud;

my son Joseph Laymon Cloud (who joined the

Heavenly Throng on February 13, 2007);

and my son David Bliss Cloud.

Contents

Waiting in Stress, Sorrow, or Fear

Waiting for Healing, Hope, Clarity

Waiting for Change

Acknowledgments

I am deeply grateful to my friend Tracey McCartney, a real computer expert, for helping get my prayers in order, for formatting my manuscript, and for getting the complete manuscript onto a CD.

It has been a real pleasure to work on this book, from idea to completed manuscript, with Robin Pippin, acquisitions editor for Upper Room Books; and with Jeannie Crawford-Lee, associate editor. Robin and Jeannie, thanks for your cheerful attitude, your practical suggestions, and for helping to broaden my vision of how this book might best serve its readers.

Contributors

Martha P. Ainsworth, LCSW, is a licensed psychotherapist in private practice in Nashville, Tennessee.

Bill Barnes was a United Methodist pastor in inner-city Nashville for thirty-four years. He was founding pastor of Edgehill United Methodist Church (in 1966), and retired in 1996.

Tommy Bugg is a manufacturer's representative. As a lay minister, he is a longtime visitor to prisoners, including those on death row.

L. R. DeMarco is an attorney with Rutherford & DeMarco, and has been practicing law in Nashville for thirty-four years.

Kathy Halbrooks lives and works in Nashville. She writes: "I enjoy the lovely landscape in Tennessee, where waiting often lends peacefulness."

Hoyt L. Hickman is a retired United Methodist minister living in Los Altos, California. He was formerly director of Worship Resource Development for the United Methodist General Board of Discipleship.

Keith McCartney is a retired U.S. Fish and Wildlife Service law enforcement officer, with over thirty-three years of experience as a wildlife conservationist.

Bruce C. Mosher is a retired broadcast journalist, radio/TV producer, media consultant, and editor.

Dorothy J. Mosher is a mother, volunteer, poet, candle maker, and baker of Communion bread.

Roela Victoria Rivera, DMin, is an educator, communications specialist, and diaconal minister in the Tennessee Conference of The United Methodist Church. She served as editor-coordinator of the Centennial book *Methodism in the Philippines: A Century of Faith and Vision.*

Michael Russell has taught college, been a college chaplain, and served as a senior editor with a Christian publisher before going on long-term medical leave.

Eugene TeSelle, a Presbyterian minister, is a professor emeritus at Vanderbilt Divinity School, in Nashville, Tennessee.

John Trainer, a licensed professional mental health counselor, practices at the Middle Tennessee Treatment Center in Nashville. He writes: "I became a born-again Christian in September, 2004, and can personally attest to God's healing grace and the power of prayer."

Laura E. Valentine is a poet-in-residence at the Penuel Ridge Retreat Center in Ashland City, Tennessee. She has cared for the dying as a hospice bedside care volunteer for more than twenty years.

Frank E. Wier and his wife, Leslie, married fifty-six years, lived in a thirty-year-old authentic log house among towering trees in the Great Smoky Mountains. Frank is a retired minister and editor for The United Methodist Church.

Susan Ford Wiltshire, professor of classics emerita at Vanderbilt University, is author of six books, including *Seasons of Grief and Grace: A Sister's Story of AIDS.*

Times
of Waiting—
Opportunities
for Prayer

A First Word to the Reader

MANY OF US have a favorite prayer book that we carry around in a jacket pocket or in a purse and pull out when we sit down to wait, for example, in a hospital, a doctor's office, or an airport waiting room. The prayers have become familiar and often bring us comfort, encouragement, or peace of mind.

Waiting may become such a book for you—at least until you have read all its prayers and, hopefully, have received some blessings from its out-of-the-ordinary pleas to the Almighty. Prayers without a byline are my offerings, and those from the contributors carry their name below the title.

The basic intention of this book is *to help you develop a mind-set:* to recognize times of waiting not as an irritating, sometimes aggravating, diversion from your planned day's activities but as *an opportunity to pray and to listen for an inkling of God's living word for you in that situation.*

How can you develop that mind-set? Consider the following four steps. First, deliberately calm down; ask God for peace of mind, peace of heart, peace of soul. Push aside your mind's clamor to get on about your planned business.

Second, look at the larger picture. How many other people are having to cope with the same delay? What problems might it pose for them?

Third, who is trying to overcome the problem causing the delay? What supportive prayers might you offer on their behalf?

Finally, when the cause of the delay is overcome, express gratitude for God's presence with all of you throughout this experience, and for God's unfailing love for you in the present moment.

Taking this approach can mean that times of waiting are not periods lost from your life but another mode of fellowship with God, who is always present, always active. This book can also serve as a springboard for your own personalized prayers.

No Time for Prayer?
John Trainer

NOW I COULD understand, in the course of our busy days, that it often seems there is precious little time to read and study God's Word; but *no time for prayer*?

Perhaps the perceived difficulty lies in the effort involved in having to think about what to say. Now that is understandable, especially if one feels obliged to come up with specific prayers for specific situations. That can certainly add more stress to the need and desire to pray—in the moment. I don't profess to know any better than the next person what the "perfect" prayer is. Or the most effective prayer in the eyes of God. But I can tell you what has been working for me, working well and quickly.

I learned this prayer from the monks of the Abbey of Gethsemani in Kentucky. They learned it from the Dutch theologian Henri Nouwen. But it is not even original with him. It has been used for generations by believers around the globe. It is timeless, easy to remember, transformative, powerful, and it is only seven words. And, if these seven words are repeated over and over, says Nouwen, eventually your heart will say it for you and the prayer itself will continue to pray within you as you work. All of your mental preoccupations and concerns should become prayer when they descend into your heart and enter the healing presence of God and become transformed by Him into His own heart.

Only seven words: *Lord Jesus Christ, have mercy on me.*

Try it. Over and over and over.

Waiting Time
Hoyt Hickman

IN A BOOK TITLED *A Day of Rest: Creating Spiritual Space in Your Week,* writer Martha Whitmore Hickman asks, "How do you use your waiting time? Do you spend precious moments waiting for a phone call? Waiting for someone to pick you up? Waiting for it to stop snowing or for the cake to come out of the oven? Instead of inwardly spinning wheels of frustration, try taking a few slow deep breaths, letting mind and body and spirit coalesce in a moment of stillness in an otherwise busy day. It is quite possible the irritating aspects of the situation will diminish if not disappear. There is another kind of waiting, which is really not waiting as much as it is honoring an inner prompting."

Hickman goes on to describe this other kind of waiting, which she calls "stepping out of the expected stream of life to honor an inner prompting." To illustrate this type of waiting, she quotes and comments on an article in *The New Yorker*, "Fall from Grace: How Modern Life Has Made Waiting a Desperate Act," in which Noelle Oxenhandler tells about a five-year-old girl learning that she was adopted.

[The adoptive father recounts,] "She didn't cry. She didn't say a word. She went into our bedroom. She climbed onto our bed and curled up at the foot of it. She lay there, in fetal position, for the entire afternoon." Oxenhandler goes on to say that she has always remembered the story and the sureness with which the child took care of herself. . . . Surely a time of Sabbath for this child—and for the adoptive parents who had the wisdom to stand away and let her make the journey only she could make.

Waiting for the Other Voice

Hoyt Hickman

WE MAY THINK of prayer as a dialogue with God, but in practice we often treat it as a monologue. We pour out our prayers. Then, if we neither get what we pray for nor hear a voice out of the blue, we may give up and consider our prayer unanswered. Perhaps we do not know how to listen and wait for the other voice in the dialogue of prayer. God may speak to us in the course of outward events or in inner promptings. A crucial part of prayer is being sensitive and imaginative enough to be aware of these as the other voice we are listening for.

Suppose I am praying for a job or searching for God's calling in my life. I start looking around me. A rejection can be understood as the closing of a door—a message that this is not the path for me. An unexpected opportunity that I could easily have missed can be understood as the opening of a door—an invitation to walk boldly through it. An inner impulse that a less attentive person might ignore may be that other voice speaking to us.

While this other voice may come quickly, it may also come only after patient waiting on our part. It may lead us to what we were praying for, or it may redirect our prayers in ways we could not have anticipated. It may take long waiting and the nurture of our power of imagination to bring us to the point where we can perceive this other voice. What we are praying for, or what we should be praying for, may take time to come to fruition.

Meanwhile, if we must persistently wait, we can remember that we could not seek God if God had not already found us and prompted our seeking. God is closer than we think, closer even than our breathing.

Waiting as a
Spiritual Discipline

WHEN WE WERE children riding in the family car to visit our grandparents, we asked frequently, "Are we almost there?" And in the Yuletide season, we asked often with eagerness, "Is it Christmas yet?"

Many Americans value speed—in cars, trains, and airplanes. Delays often make us impatient. Slow-moving traffic or traffic jams are the excuse for some persons to give way to "road rage," sometimes resulting in wrecks, injuries, or even deaths.

Waiting in long lines to fill our cars with gas or to have our basket of groceries checked out makes many of us fidget or mutter our displeasure. A visitor from a slower-paced society might think, "Americans are impatient people!"

This tendency toward impatience is present for many of us in our spiritual lives as well as in our physical lives. We pray for healing of loved ones that may come slowly, if at all. We pray for an end to wars that kill thousands of human beings but drag on year after year. We pray for jobs that are stressfully slow in materializing or that are outsourced to other nations. Where is God in these painful circumstances? Does God really care what happens to human beings? "How long, O Lord?" we cry out in anguish.

Turning to scriptures, we hear counsel that speaks to this widespread and painful spiritual quandary. The prophet Isaiah wrote:

Those who wait for the LORD shall renew
    their strength,
    they shall mount up with wings like
      eagles,
    they shall run and not be weary,
they shall walk and not faint. (Isa. 40:31)

This is Isaiah's inspiring promise of spiritual renewal, of reaching new heights of insight and faith, and God's gift to persons who are expectantly waiting. Further, Isaiah speaks of the energy and ability to persevere as they move toward their goals. Isn't this passage a strong motivation for us to learn to "wait for the LORD"?

David models patience in waiting for an awareness of God, for a personal encounter with God:

Lead me in your truth, and teach me,
    for you are the God of my salvation;
    for you I wait all day long. (Ps. 25:5)

How many of us today can say, "For you I wait all day long"? Another psalmist writes:

I wait for the LORD, my soul waits,
    and in his word I hope;
my soul waits for the Lord
    more than those who watch for the
        morning. (Ps. 130:5-6)

This is not just a resigned or grudging mental and spiritual exercise. Rather, the psalmist's experience is characterized by hope and eagerness.

Isaiah, like the psalmist, waits with an attitude of hope for God's self-disclosure, which will come in God's own time:

I will wait for the Lord, who is hiding his face from the house of Jacob, and I will hope in him. (Isa. 8:17)

The prophet Hosea counsels his hearers to wait while holding fast to love and justice:

Return to your God,
hold fast to love and justice,
and wait continually for your God.
(Hos. 12:6)

In modern lingo, Hosea is saying, "Don't get impatient and give up on God, but persevere in your waiting." All these passages of scripture underline the truth that our prayer life should include both a quest for personal holiness and a commitment to working faithfully for social justice.

Waiting
in Gratitude

Introduction
Gratitude Is a
Two-Way Street

MY FIRST PROFESSOR of theology in seminary, Dr. Edward T. Ramsdell, stated with conviction, "Gratitude is the most profound emotion of which we human beings are capable." I've remembered that across the years and have asked myself, *Why did he say that? Is that statement justified?*

The World Book Dictionary defines *gratitude* as "a kindly feeling because of a favor received; desire to do a favor in return; thankfulness." Turning to the Bible, we find many passages in the Psalms, the Gospels, the Acts, the Letters, and the Revelation, urging us to "give thanks to the Lord" and to "come into [God's] presence with thanksgiving." This is the right response of human beings to our Creator, Sustainer, and Savior, who gives us all of life's blessings and—

supremely—eternal life through Jesus Christ's gift of his life for us on the Cross.

Because Jesus Christ gave himself for us unstintingly, we want to follow his commandment and love one another as he loved us (see 1 John 4:7-12). Gratitude is a two-way street: we receive God's gifts, and we show our thankfulness by being channels of God's love to our fellow human beings, especially those in need and often rejected by society. (See Matt. 25:31-46.)

Waiting to Receive Communion

O GOD, FATHER of our Lord and Savior Jesus Christ,

Here I wait to receive the bread and wine, in the company of fellow Christians. My heart is full to overflowing with gratitude as, once more, I try to comprehend the unimaginable love you poured out on the human family by sending your Son into the world to show us the Way to eternal life.

The broken bread and the wine remind me of Jesus' excruciating death on the Cross, which he suffered willingly to make clear that God's love has no limits.

How can I show my gratitude to you, God? How can I open the minds and hearts of persons who have not yet discovered the love you long to pour out on their lives? I will be quiet, O Lord, and listen for any living words that you might have for me as I wait to receive Communion. Amen.

Waiting for Sleep to Come

GOD OF CONSTANT, universal awareness,

The psalmist was confident that the God "who keeps Israel will neither slumber nor sleep" (Ps. 121:4). That is one of the most glaring differences between the infinite God and us finite creatures. For at the end of an eventful day, filled with work and perhaps some upsetting encounters, we are worn out and long for nothing so much as a good night's sleep.

But sometimes, O God, our minds keep whirling and refuse to shut down. Recently, I experienced such a night; I decided not to fight it but instead to reflect quietly on my long life. Being still, being quiet, my mind and heart opened wide to memories from early childhood to now. A hundred friends—or more—welled up clearer than paintings on my bedroom walls.

As I lay reviewing this family-and-friends parade, many on the other side of death, I was bathed in gratitude for all the love this kid from Arkansas has received as gift in one lifetime.

Early morning hours, before even neighborhood birds begin to chirp, invite review of relationships: first loves, marriages, work and achievements, parenting's problems and rewards.

Too old now for excuses—time for a reality check. God's grace and goodness bring tears to my eyes and a smile to my lips.

Finally, sleep. Thank you, Lord! Amen.

Waiting to "Set My Affairs in Order"

Eugene TeSelle

O GOD, THE GIVER of all good things,

I give thanks to you, O God, for all the days of my life, which may stretch out to threescore and ten, or fourscore, or even more. May I live out my life with gratitude, looking to you for all that I need and not being anxious about tomorrow.

But what if I should turn out to be like the rich fool who has laid up supplies for many years but suddenly finds that his soul is required of him this very night? We have been told to qualify our plans by always adding, "God willing."

Perhaps that seems morbid, a holdover from an era when life was much riskier. I have tried to be a good steward of your gifts. I have not buried my talents but put them to use, and they have borne fruit. I must continue being a steward, not only out of gratitude to you but for the benefit of others who depend on me.

I have so much to be grateful for—home, possessions, savings, heirlooms and inheritances, memorabilia and documents and jottings, books that I still value, and so many objects that I might still find useful. Even the thought of sorting through all these things is painful. It would be like killing my memories before their time, sending them to oblivion.

And yet I am the one who should do it. There is much that might be useful to me sometime in the future, but much deserves oblivion. Some of these possessions are trivial; some are embarrassing; some are even worse than that.

When I put myself in the place of those who will try to go through all these things, I can't help but pity them. How could they find their way through all my possessions? How could they begin to trace my bank accounts or the organizations in which I have responsibilities or the friends who would want to know about my death?

Considering this prospect reminds me of all the stories about people who did not have a will, or did not update it, causing confusion for their relatives. It reminds me of the houses I have seen standing empty, and sometimes boarded up, because inheritance is uncertain.

Keep me from denial, avoidance, or procrastination, O God. Give me resoluteness for what I know will be a difficult task. There are some things that should be given to others, right now. There are some things that should be given to a church, a library, or a historical society.

You are the one who gives us all good things. This means that in life, in death, and in life beyond death, we belong to you. May I continue to look to you, wherever I should be in that pilgrimage. Only then can I say that I have left a worthy heritage behind me. Being aware of all of this, may I run with perseverance the race that is set before me, looking to Jesus, the pioneer and perfecter of our faith. Amen.

Waiting in Line at a Post Office

O GOD, THE GREAT communicator,

In all centuries you have sought to communicate your loving will for humankind through prophets, lawgivers, psalmists, and letter writers.

Here we are today in this post office, intent on communicating with friends, relatives, organizations, and businesses.

Some of the parcels contain books that we have found helpful and which we want to share with friends or relatives.

Some are applying for passports. May they travel safely and have gratifying encounters with persons in other countries; and may their eyes be open to the beautiful landscapes and seascapes they will see. May their new experiences stretch their minds and hearts and challenge them to work for world peace.

Some are buying stamps to send greetings to friends for Thanksgiving, Christmas, Hanukkah, Easter, birthdays, graduations, weddings, and anniversaries; others to express sympathy on the loss of loved ones.

Positive communication knits us together as families, as communities, as nations, and as a world. I am grateful for the functions that the post office performs. Bless the postal employees in their work.

Amen.

Waiting for Our Car to Be Repaired

O GOD, WHO MAKES all things new,

We rejoice that you renew the earth after hurricanes, earthquakes, floods, and droughts. We are grateful that you renew our bodies as we eat healthy diets, exercise, and get proper rest. We live in an age of many machines, including automobiles; we recognize that in time they inevitably wear out or break down.

We depend on cars for many useful functions: to visit family and friends, to go to Sunday school and church, to go to grocery stores, to get to offices or other places of work, to visit persons in hospitals and prisons. A car enables us to do more in a day's time than our ancestors could with their horses and buggies.

When our car breaks down, we tend to become irritated and impatient. But as we sit in the garage's waiting room, we can "be still and know that (you) are God." We give thanks for mechanics who repair our car and "get us back on the road."

We pray for all the other people who are waiting for their cars to be repaired. When they leave, may they—and we—drive safely and respect the rights of all other drivers on the highway.

Thank you, Heavenly Father, for your loving presence with us wherever we may be. Amen.

Waiting in Line at the Grocery Store

Martha Ainsworth

HEAVENLY FATHER,

Thank you for all of your blessings. Thank you that because of your grace, I have the resources to feed my family and myself. Forgive me when I do not recognize this for the gift that it is. Please have mercy on those here and in the world who are hungry and starving. For those of us who have been given so much, provide us with the strength and the resolve to reach out a helping hand so that we may be instruments of your love. These things I ask in Christ's name. Amen.

Waiting for Daybreak

Roela Victoria Rivera

WITH GREAT JOY in my heart,
I praise and thank you, God,
for this new day and new light,
for new hope and new strength.

With great faith and hope in my heart,
may this new day spring and bring
new blessing and new beginning
that will guide us throughout the day.

Bless my loved ones near and far away.
May we follow your will and way
in everything we do and say.

Thank you for the gift of this new day.
Whatever we do today
is our humble offering. Thank you, God,
    for everything.

Waiting for Openness to the Beauty of God's Creation

Keith McCartney

DEAR GOD, THANK YOU so much for creating such an amazing world for us to live in. When we take time simply to look around us, we see an astounding number of examples of your love for us. Please help us not to take these for granted. Guide us and our leaders to truly appreciate your world and not to continue on the path of destroying it, as we seem inclined to do. Lord, your proof of love is everywhere. Truly, how could we *not* believe? For it is in Jesus' name that we ask these things. Amen.

Waiting with a
Psalm: Psalm 103

Of David.

BLESS THE LORD, O my soul,
    and all that is within me,
    bless his holy name.
Bless the LORD, O my soul,
    and do not forget all his benefits—
who forgives all your iniquity,
    who heals all your diseases,
who redeems your life from the Pit,
    who crowns you with steadfast love
        and mercy,
who satisfies you with good as long as
    you live
    so that your youth is renewed like
        the eagle's.

The LORD works vindication
    and justice for all who are oppressed.

He made known his ways to Moses,
　　his acts to the people of Israel.
The Lord is merciful and gracious,
　　slow to anger and abounding in stead-
　　　　fast love.
He will not always accuse,
　　nor will he keep his anger forever.
He does not deal with us according to
　　our sins,
　　nor repay us according to our
　　　　iniquities.
For as the heavens are high above
　　the earth,
　　so great is his steadfast love toward
　　　　those who fear him;
as far as the east is from the west,
　　so far he removes our transgressions
　　　　from us.
As a father has compassion for his children,
　　so the Lord pities those who fear him.
For he knows how we were made;
　　he remembers that we are dust.

As for mortals, their days are like grass;
　　they flourish like a flower of the field;

for the wind passes over it, and it is gone,
    and its place knows it no more.
But the steadfast love of the LORD is from
    everlasting to everlasting
    on those who fear him,
    and his righteousness to children's
        children,
to those who keep his covenant
    and remember to do his command-
        ments.
The LORD has established his throne in the
    heavens,
    and his kingdom rules over all.
Bless the LORD, O you his angels,
    you mighty ones who do his bidding,
obedient to his spoken word.
Bless the LORD, all his hosts,
    his ministers that do his will.
Bless the LORD, all his works,
    in all places of his dominion.
Bless the LORD, O my soul.

Waiting in the Present Moment

Tommy Bugg

O GOD, WHAT A beauty you give! This day, full of sunshine, white clouds, and deep blue sky; that snowy, cold day; or that dark rainy day. There is a light that shines beyond all of humankind's visual expectations—a light so bright as to fill even the darkest heart. A brilliant light so full of love that it can reach to the deepest, most sinful soul!

Thank you, God, for showing me your light of love, your eternal peace.

O God, this is the present; yet it is so fleeting. To dwell with you now and in every thought is so difficult, yet you should be the center of our universe. This one life with you, O God, is the one that will last down through the ages. Everything else is just smoke; for when the end comes, then comes the true beginning. Thank you, God, for this—your moment, our moment—in time. Amen.

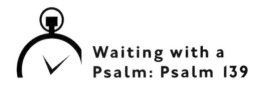

Waiting with a Psalm: Psalm 139

To the leader. Of David. A Psalm.

O LORD, YOU HAVE searched me and
   known me.
You know when I sit down and when I rise
   up;
   you discern my thoughts from far away.
You search out my path and my lying
   down,
   and are acquainted with all my ways.
Even before a word is on my tongue,
   O LORD, you know it completely.
You hem me in, behind and before,
   and lay your hand upon me.
Such knowledge is too wonderful for me;
   it is so high that I cannot attain it.

Where can I go from your spirit?
   Or where can I flee from your presence?
If I ascend to heaven, you are there;

if I make my bed in Sheol, you are
     there.
If I take the wings of the morning
     and settle at the farthest limits of
          the sea,
even there your hand shall lead me,
     and your right hand shall hold me fast.
If I say, "Surely the darkness shall cover me,
     and the light around me become
          night,"
even the darkness is not dark to you;
     the night is as bright as the day,
     for darkness is as light to you.

For it was you who formed my
          inward parts;
     you knit me together in my mother's
          womb.
I praise you, for I am fearfully and
          wonderfully made.
     Wonderful are your works;
that I know very well.
     My frame was not hidden from you,
when I was being made in secret,
     intricately woven in the depths of
          the earth.

Your eyes beheld my unformed substance.
In your book were written
all the days that were formed for me,
when none of them as yet existed.
How weighty to me are your thoughts, O
God!
How vast is the sum of them!
I try to count them—they are more than
the sand;
I come to the end—I am still with you.

O that you would kill the wicked, O God,
and that the bloodthirsty would depart
from me—
those who speak of you maliciously,
and lift themselves up against you for
evil!
Do I not hate those who hate you, O Lord?
And do I not loathe those who rise up
against you?
I hate them with perfect hatred;
I count them my enemies.
Search me, O God, and know my heart;
test me and know my thoughts.
See if there is any wicked way in me,
and lead me in the way everlasting.

Waiting in Personal Thanksgiving

L. R. DeMarco

DEAR LORD, THANK YOU for all the good things you have provided in my life. I have many blessings that I too often take for granted. I thank you for these and for the many people you have chosen to be with me in life's journey. I thank you too for those things in my life that you have provided as challenges and trials for me to overcome. I thank you for good health, both physical and mental, and pray that you will continue to bless me. I thank you most of all for your unconditional and eternal love. Amen.

Waiting in
Stress, Sorrow,
or Fear

Introduction
When Life Squeezes a Painful Prayer Out of Us

YOU PROBABLY KNOW the saying that emerged in wartime: "There are no atheists in foxholes!" That grew out of the experiences of millions of soldiers, sailors, and airmen who found themselves terrified by ear-shattering explosions of bombs, gunfire, flamethrowers, and screaming enemies. Feeling utterly powerless and fearing that they might be just moments from dismemberment or death, GIs cried out: "O God, help me! Help me, please!"

Sadly, sixty-five years after the conclusion of World War II, American men and women are again caught up in vicious warfare in several countries. And it is not just today's servicemen and women who cry out in spiritual anguish but their spouses, children, parents, and friends as well. In a number of places, entire congregations have committed themselves to pray for these men and women from their congregation or town.

Not only war but also painful diseases that resist medical treatment drive many persons to anguished prayer. As a parent, I can empathize with parents of afflicted children from infancy to adulthood. The magnitude of the problem is highlighted by the fact that entire hospitals are filled with children who are quite sick. And, as we stretch our minds to think globally, we are almost overwhelmed by the knowledge that millions of children in Africa are suffering with AIDS, and other millions are dying of hunger.

Even as we support health and anti-hunger organizations to address these problems, we cannot suppress an occasional groan. The magnitude of evil in the world drives us to our knees in anguished prayer, knowing in our hearts that this is God's world and that God is at work in it to overcome evil with good. But like an ancient prophet, we cry out, "How long, O Lord?"

When we are waiting in stress, sorrow, or fear, it is important *to pray with some specificity*. Why? Because as we try to comprehend the dimensions of the problem we are wrestling with, we might begin to get an inkling as to what we can do, working with God, to help solve the problem.

Some of us have the spiritual problem of *impatience*. It is hard for us to listen quietly, and at length, for the "still small voice" of God that might give insight and direction for as we confront difficult situations. So we can *pray for patience*, confident that God will answer our prayers—in God's own way and time. May your times of waiting be spiritually productive.

Waiting for Power to Be Restored

CREATOR OF HEAVEN and Earth,

Most of the time we rejoice in the beauty of the world you have created and feel our spirits lifted by the changing of the seasons. Most of the time we are grateful for earth's fecundity that yields bountiful crops, adequate not only to supply our needs but also to ship many tons of food to other nations.

But sometimes, tremendous storms blow from ocean to shore and inland, destroying trees and the homes of hundreds of families. Sometimes rain comes down in heavy sheets of water, causing creeks and rivers to overflow, flooding whole towns.

We know about this firsthand, O Lord. Strong winds broke big tree limbs that fell on electric lines and knocked out power to thousands of families. We've been without power for five days. We're so used to having the use of all the appliances powered by electricity that we feel almost helpless. Be with us and with all our neighbors, O Lord, as we try to cope with these problems.

We hear the constant buzz of chain saws. Workers are laboring to clear up the tangle of trees and repair electric lines. Give these workers strength as they toil hard for long hours to restore power to our homes.

As we wait for power to be restored, we are mindful that life is precarious; sudden and unexpected changes in the earth's environment can upset what we thought was safe and secure. But remind us, O Lord, that you are with us in every circumstance of life, that you love us perfectly, and that you expect us to help one another—however overwhelming problems might seem at the time—in the spirit of Christ. Amen.

Waiting for a Friend to Die

O GOD, OUR REFUGE and strength,

Our hearts are full of sadness and pain as we watch our dear friend losing strength. It appears that his body's systems are closing down one by one.

We remember with gratitude all those months and years when he was full of health and good cheer, and we thank you that we were able to share life and laughter with him. It comforts our hearts to know that you, our loving heavenly Father, are with him right now, this very day. We know that whether we live or whether we die, we are the Lord's children, the sheep of his pasture.

In faith we lift up our dear friend into your presence for blessing. May he know, in the core of his being, that you love him perfectly, and that we love him as he is.

All this we pray in the name of our Lord Jesus Christ, who died and rose again to open our hearts and minds to the reality of eternal life with you. Amen.

Waiting for a Loved One to Die

Laura E. Valentine

O GOD, YOU FEEL so distant as I wait for my loved one to die. I pray [*Name*] will soon be released from the burden of this earthly existence, but I am sad, I am angry, and I am afraid. I don't know what to do or say as [*Name*] journeys from this life to the next. Where is your mercy, God, as I grieve?

Great Creator, who has promised us life eternal, soothe my pain, relieve this gnawing sense of loss. Enable me to be a witness to your grace as nurses and caregivers lay gentle and compassionate hands on my loved one who is dying. Help me see your face in the face of family and friends who gather around the bed to say good-bye. O God, let us be fully present to one another and to the miracle of this sacred life as it passes before us.

Amen.

Waiting to Be Called Home

Frank E. Wier (for a friend)

O LORD, YOU HAVE answered my prayers for long life and a sound mind. Now I am ninety-eight years old, and I don't want to live any longer. I am in pain, always in pain.

My friends all try to encourage me, saying, "Oh, you'll live to be a hundred." I don't want to be a hundred. Someone brought me a silly album of interviews with centenarians. Supposed to have wisdom. They didn't have any wisdom. *I* don't have wisdom. I don't have any consolation for being old and tired and in pain.

I lie on my couch and nod and snooze all day, and then I lie awake all night. In the day I welcome my guests. They love me; they haven't forgotten me. But not one of them has the guts to say, "I'm praying for you to die." Why not? Don't they believe you are there to welcome me?

Tonight, like every night, I am awake. I

am blind and deaf, but I sing the hymns that I have had so many years to memorize. I recite the psalms that I love: "O LORD, thou hast searched me and known me. . . . even the darkness is not dark to thee" (Ps. 139:1, 12, RSV). I'm an old English teacher, and I make up word games—beautiful, interesting words, for classes I will never teach. And I face the awful threat: *tomorrow is another day!*

The last thing I worry about is dying. Why can't I go home? Please, good Lord, Father of mercies, take me home! Amen.

Waiting for Employment after Losing a Job

O GOD, OUR LOVING heavenly Parent, we know that Jesus told his followers,

> Do not worry, saying "What will we eat?" or "What will we drink?" or "What will we wear?" . . . your heavenly Father knows that you need all these things. But strive first for the kingdom of God and his righteousness, and all these things will be given to you as well. (Matt. 6:31-33)

Jesus' teaching really strains my faith, God! The world we live in today is much more complex than it was two thousand years ago. Shifts of manufacturing to other nations throws thousands of people out of work at one time, stripping us of jobs that we thought were secure until our retirement. How can we *not* worry? Is it naive to believe that "God will provide"? What does it mean to "strive first for the kingdom of God" in these circumstances?

Holy Spirit, open my mind, my heart, and my will to obey Jesus' teaching—even though I can't see clearly how to do so. Guide me in this time of radical change, and enable me to trust your goodness for me and for my fellow workers, even before we find new jobs. Amen.

Waiting for a War to End

O GOD, WHOSE WILL is peace on Earth,

Our hearts are heavy with grief when we witness scenes of death and destruction daily on TV. We know—and have known for centuries—that war is hell. Yet we frantically push ahead, vainly trying to end the war with more violence, more tanks and guns, more soldiers—who are killed or injured by the thousands.

Open our minds and hearts so that we will believe—and act on—Jesus' teaching: "Blessed are the peacemakers, for they will be called children of God" (Matt. 5:9). Guide our actions and give us strength to persevere until hatred is replaced by mutual understanding, respect, and love. Then we shall have peace. Amen.

Waiting for Road Rage to Subside

Susan Ford Wiltshire

IT ALL STARTED with our daughter.

She and I used to park in a reserved place next to a woman who once left a peremptory note on my windshield with a request, entirely justified, that I improve my parking skills. One day Carrie said, "Oh, Mom, it's all right, she has to leave during lunch every day to take her daughter to dialysis." Soon the story ramped up in tone: "This time she has gone to the doctor to plan how she can donate one of her kidneys to her daughter. And her husband isn't a bit supportive. This must be very hard for her."

That experience started me on storytelling when I am annoyed behind the wheel in traffic. I often say—out loud, whether I have passengers or not—something like "Oh, honey, I know it's been a hard day for you. Your wife is threatening to leave you and you can't pay your credit card bill, and you're afraid your son is on drugs. Your mother-in-law is mad at you too. I am so sorry."

Or maybe I intone as follows: "Bless your heart. Your mind is thousands of miles away with your husband in Iraq, and you don't like your job, and the children are acting out, and there's not enough money. It must be incredibly hard for you just to go get groceries."

Usually by the time my story peters out, the miscreant has either passed me by or started moving at the green light.

I know my fictions help me. And maybe someday, in a pedestrian place like an elevator, I will meet someone for whom something I say will strike a spark.

Maybe that day I can help some other person too.

Waiting for a Late Plane to Arrive

O GOD OF EARTH, sea, and sky,

Millions of us travel frequently—on business, on vacation, or to visit family and friends. When we stop to reflect on this fact, we affirm that we are always in your hands, whether on the earth, on the sea, or in the sky. We also have confidence that drivers, sea captains, and pilots are skilled and will take us safely to our destination.

But we also are aware that sometimes weather conditions or mechanical failures cause accidents that result in injuries—or even death—for a number of passengers.

Here in this airport, family members and friends have a measure of anxiety for the well-being of loved ones on a plane that is running quite late. Has the plane run into a storm? Has a mechanical failure of some kind forced it down in another city for repairs? Or, worst of all, has it crashed into a mountainside or into the ocean? We pray that your Spirit will bring comfort and peace of mind to each of us waiting here.

O God, we pray for all the passengers on that plane—not just for our loved one. Relieve their stress or anxiety. We pray for the pilot and crew of that plane; give them wisdom and resourcefulness in meeting whatever challenge they face that has delayed their flight. And we pray that, even though the plane is late, it will soon arrive safely at this airport. Amidst all the joyful greetings, remind us to give you our deep thanks and praise! Amen.

Waiting for a Mammogram

Dorothy J. Mosher

THERE'S NO REASON I should be
  fearful, God. Every other year my test
  was normal.
So, why am I so jumpy?
The other people waiting may have the
  same feelings.
One couple—elderly—passive.
The husband leans lovingly in her
  direction.
Please, God, help them still their thudding
  thoughts, to face unpleasantness if
  that's the verdict.
We are all fragile children.
The door opens; my name is called.
Be with me, God, and with all who
  gather here.
Amen.

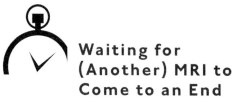

Waiting for (Another) MRI to Come to an End

Michael Russell

O ABIDING PRESENCE,

Can you hear me? In this coffinlike tunnel, engulfed by jackhammer-like sounds, I'm not sure we can communicate. I know you are with me; I feel your presence. *But can you hear me? God?*

Faith is called for, trust. Given my diagnosis—an illness debilitating but not life-threatening—I can summon a measure of confidence. But what of others tested in this machine today, those who face more critical circumstances? *Can you hear them, Lord God?*

And what about my friend Bryan, struggling to speak after his brain injury? And Connie, all alone to deal with the aftermath of her father's death? And Vincent, so frail at eighty-nine but caring for Dorothy, his "older woman" for almost seventy years, her spirit shining with the Light but her body growing dimmer day by day? O God, these are good people! Wonderful people! People who have blessed the world—have blessed me—with laughter, collegiality, counsel, music, prayer.

Ensconced in this medical marvel, left to my own devices, I recall the voices of these dear friends—*I can hear them, Lord, albeit indistinctly, even deep in this chamber, above this cacophony! And you, Lord, must hear them also—perfectly!* You must hear Bryan and Connie and Vincent and Dorothy in their trying situations, must hear each of the other be-gowned subjects who have been nor will be tested in this MRI today, must hear . . . me.

Ah, my God, once again I encounter you through the voices of others. Even in this place, within this ambiance, you and I converse by means of their testimonies. I am grateful, my Lord, grateful.

Amen.

Waiting to Sell Our House

Dorothy J. Mosher

HERE WE ARE, God, waiting.
Waiting along with several thousand
    others.
We see the For Sale signs as we drive along
on busy streets and quiet lanes.

We are waiting, God,
because there is nothing we can do
    except wait.
Wait till the perfect buyer comes
who "loves this house"
and has the stash to pay the earnest
    money.

Meanwhile, we dust and clean
and straighten bookshelves.
Put fresh flowers in the bowl,
waiting for someone,
waiting for action,
waiting for release.

We know you are with us, God,
but it feels so lonely.
Give us the sense of your loving presence.
Assure us that we are not alone.
Amen.

Waiting for a Runaway Youth to Come Home

FATHER/MOTHER GOD,

From Jesus' story about the prodigal son (Luke 15:11-32) we know that your heart, like ours, longs for loving relationship to be restored with our child who has run away from home. We have agonized through many anxious days and restless nights. Our imagination often makes us fearful about what could happen to our beloved daughter [or, son].

We pray that you will surround with loving care and keep him/her from harm. May caring adults provide food, shelter, and friendship to our child, so that this time apart—so painful for us parents—will not be destructive physically, mentally, or spiritually.

O Spirit of God, plant in the mind and heart of our child the knowledge that we love her/him deeply and pray constantly for her/him to return home. There will be a warm welcome and a joyful reunion. Amen.

Waiting for Dignity in Prison

Frank E. Wier (for a friend)

DEAR JESUS, MY MOM and dad taught me to pray to you, and I know that you answer. Thank you for answering. I told you already what I did that brought me here, to this state prison. It was very bad, and I am paying for it.

I'm almost fifty, and if I ever get out, I'll be at least seventy-five. I don't even think about it. My mom and dad will be gone. My brothers and sisters will be old. My nieces and nephews will not know me. I am missing everything about their growing up. So time is nothing. I'm not waiting to get out.

The guards are scared of us, so they holler and curse and jerk us around to make us scared of them. I'm a number to them. The chaplain knows my name. I have some friends. But I am almost not a person at all. *That's what I am waiting for: to be a person again.* Any chance? Can you help me?

The state wants to forget me. But this is my only life. I deserve to be punished, but I don't deserve to be nothing, do I? Did you ever feel that you were just nothing at all, when they punished you? Help me, Lord, to be at least something. A person, at least. Thank you. Amen.

Waiting for Healing and Waiting for Death

Part 1
Waiting for Healing for My Son's Three Major Illnesses

O JESUS CHRIST, the Great Physician,

During your earthly ministry, out of your compassion you healed persons of all kinds of diseases. I believe you are present and active today and that you love Joe perfectly. Dear Lord, work through all the doctors, nurses, technicians, pastors, and family members who are trying to help Joe fully recover from rheumatoid arthritis that has crippled his hands. What a cruel turn of fate for a young man who has been a master mechanic as well as a good golfer and baseball player!

Living Christ, heal and strengthen Joe's heart. His pacemaker and defibrillator help, but please prevent another heart attack.

Lord, help Joe recover from the stroke that has limited his use of one arm and that has garbled his speech.

When Joe's pain in his hands, feet, neck, shoulders, and back is unendurable, he calls me—often in the middle of the night—to come up to his room and massage him. I gladly go; but he usually says, "I'm sorry, Dad, to get you out of bed." I reassure him: "Joe, don't apologize! It's a *privilege* to come help you at any time." He asks: "What do you mean by 'a privilege'?" I tell him: "When you love someone, it is a privilege to do anything you can to reduce his pain and help him move toward recovery." As I massage first one part then another of his aching body, I'm silently praying, "Jesus, use my hands to communicate your love to Joe, and make them instruments of your healing power."

O steadfast Lord, give me patience as months pass and Joe's pain and total disability push him toward depression and despair. Help me to trust you, Lord, and to hold onto hope. Amen.

Part 2
Waiting for Joe to Go to God

O merciful God, all the doctors, machines, and medicines in this fine hospital seem unable to stop Joe's physical decline. He can no longer swallow anything. The liquid nutrients put into his body through an IV have caused a yeast infection in his blood, so they have been discontinued. The nurse told me a short time ago: "Joe doesn't have long to live."

I called our pastors, present and past, and they have just arrived in Joe's room. And one of Joe's best friends, by happy coincidence, has come also. I suggest that we join hands with Joe in a prayer circle; then our longtime pastor lifts Joe to God in prayer. When we open our eyes, Joe is gone. Our new pastor says: "He felt permission to go." (His doctors have been saying, "Fight, Joe, fight!" But he had no strength left to fight for health.)

I hug Joe and, as my tears stream down, I affirm, "Now Joe is in God's presence forever!" I see Joe in your loving presence, God, free of all disabilities and pain, and filled with joy. May that assurance enable us to cope with pain and grief at Joe's death. Amen.

Waiting for My Son to Win Freedom from an Addiction

O GOD, FATHER OF OUR Lord Jesus Christ:

We believe the apostle Paul when he writes: "For freedom Christ has set us free" (Gal. 5:1). We are challenged by him to "live by the Spirit . . . and do not gratify the desires of the flesh"—which include "drunkenness" (Gal. 5:16, 21).

The personal and social problem of abusive drinking, already present in the first century CE, is widespread in the twenty-first century. We are deeply troubled, O Lord, by reports of binge drinking on college campuses. Many of these young people probably believe that they can "drink or leave it alone." But, sadly, a considerable number become addicted to alcohol, which leads to physical illnesses, broken personal relationships, lost jobs, homelessness. All these eventualities cause much grief for the alcoholic's parents, siblings, spouse, and friends.

Loving Father, I know that you want my son to be freed from addiction to alcohol. Then he will be free to use his talents to the full, maintain healthy relationships with his family and friends, and regain his self-respect and self-confidence.

I am grateful for the Twelve-Step Program and other programs designed to support persons in recovering from addictions. I am truly glad that my son has recognized his need for help and has enrolled in one of these programs. I pray daily that he and all the members of his therapy group will grow in self-control and in commitment to living a life of sobriety, one day at a time. With them, I pray Reinhold Niebuhr's prayer: "God, grant me the serenity to accept the things I cannot change; the courage to change the things I can; and the wisdom to know the difference."

In hope and trust that you will be present every day with my son and his colleagues, and with my family and me, I say a heartfelt thank-you, ever-loving Father. Amen.

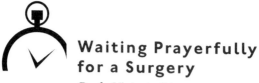

Waiting Prayerfully for a Surgery

Roela Victoria Rivera

WHILE IN A HOSPITAL holding room,
waiting for a surgical procedure,
I lie quietly and patiently,
surrendering everything to thee.

I am filled with deep anxiety,
but I trust that the Lord Almighty
will set my spirit free and take
     good care of me.

Bless the surgeon and all medical staff,
who render service professionally
and attend to patients like me.
I know and fully understand
I am in good hands and in God's hand.

Waiting
for Healing,
Hope, Clarity

Introduction
Being Watchful in a
Soporific Society

HOW OFTEN DO WE block out an extended period to think in depth about what's happening in our society and our world, to evaluate these actions in the light of Jesus' teachings and example? Pressed to tell the truth, most of us would have to answer, "Not often."

Part of the reason is the widespread clamor to be entertained. Television—with hundreds of channels—movies, and video games fill up human consciousness most of the waking hours for many citizens. Much of this fare is soporific—that is, it causes or tends to cause sleep. Our higher brain centers shut down as they are bombarded by trivial, lowest-common-denominator programs. When much of the population mindlessly floats through the days on this sea of entertainment, opportunistic individuals and groups find an opening. They can—and do—manipulate business and government for their own greedy purposes, leaving millions of Americans jobless, homeless, and without health care.

Turning this destructive pattern around will not be easy. Pundits and politicians rush forward with "bailouts," but few recommend massive change in the behavior of society that has landed us in this mess. Christians—and Jews and Muslims and secularists—rightly seek to provide emergency aid for homeless and hungry individuals and families. But the living Christ challenges us to a deeper, more permanent answer. What is it?

Earlier generations of Christians practiced *vigils*, defined as "the act of keeping awake; act of watching; a night spent in prayer." From that practice we understand that being *vigilant* means "keeping steadily on the alert; attentively or closely observant; watchful, wide-awake, or cautious."

This concept was not imposed by some later monastic or ascetic group. Jesus told his disciples, "Keep awake . . . for you do not know on what day your Lord is coming" (Matt. 24:42). He continued, "You also must be ready, for the Son of man is coming at an unexpected hour" (Matt. 24:44). And in the same extended discourse, Jesus set forth clearly the criteria for ultimate approval or disapproval by the Almighty: feeding the hungry, clothing the naked, visiting the sick and prisoners (Matt. 25:31-46).

Christians who are vigilant in the twenty-first century, who are wide awake, attentively and closely observant, will quickly recognize that we have been "asleep at the switch"—which results not only in deadly train crashes but also in meltdowns of the American economy (with huge negative impacts on the economies of many other nations) and widespread personal and family disasters.

Jesus' command to "wake up!" is directed to all Christians today. While we wait for new light to break, we must act on the best insights we have, trusting that God is with us, loving us fully and willing our salvation as individuals and as a whole society.

What should we watch for in our vigils?

- Imaginative breakthroughs of peace in a warring world, replacing traditional enmities with mutual respect and cooperation.
- Widespread and persistent programs to feed all the world's hungry children and adults; to heal the sick in every nation; to house the homeless in safe and sanitary homes; to educate the ignorant, both male and female, in all areas of knowledge; to provide meaningful employment for all of the unemployed.
- New and humane programs to control and rehabilitate youth and adults who have committed crimes, and effective programs to reintegrate them into society.
- Worldwide programs that encourage and enable people to learn about cultures other than their own, that open people's eyes to the beauty of diverse cultures.

- Worldwide commitment by all nations to take practical action to preserve earth's environment.

All these new, healthy, and inclusive dimensions of human life may be breakthrough points where the Spirit of Christ has "come again" to earth, in the invincible power of God's love, to enable all humanity to experience God's kingdom "on earth as it is in heaven" (Matt. 6:10).

Waiting for the Congregation to Assemble

O GOD, OUR MAKER and Redeemer,

On this first day of the week, the call of the ancient psalmist sounds in our minds and hearts as a gracious invitation—as pertinent today as it was when first sung more than two thousand years ago:

O come, let us worship and bow down,
  let us kneel before the LORD, our Maker!
For he is our God,
  and we are the people of his pasture,
  and the sheep of his hand. (Ps. 95:6-7)

As longtime members of this congregation, we like to arrive early and greet our fellow members as they come in. It's a joy to see a cluster of smiling young adults; already they are taking active roles in the life of the church.

We look for some older members who've been homebound for a few weeks because of illness or injury; it is always gratifying to see them return, able once again to worship with us.

We keep our eyes open for newcomers—some, students from nearby colleges; some, visitors from other states or even other nations! We want them to know that they are truly welcome.

It is a particular joy to see children arrive—toddlers with their parents, older children chatting energetically with their friends. We remind ourselves that they are *not* "the church of the future"—they are an important part of the church *today.* Jesus' firm word to his disciples sounds clearly in our minds in the twenty-first century:

> Let the little children come to me, and do not stop them; for it is to such that the kingdom of heaven belongs. (Matt. 19:14)

The bell sounds, calling us to worship. We seek to clear our mind of all distractions.

For six days, many of us have been preoccupied with our work, recreation, and family matters. Now, the imperative word of Jesus Christ brings us sharply to attention: "Worship the Lord your God, and serve only him" (Matt. 4:10).

What gets our attention, gets us! We don't want to woolgather; each hymn, each prayer, each sermon might suddenly shine a bright light on a dark corner of our personal life or on difficult problems in our community or nation.

O God, we pray that as we worship, our congregation may be filled this day with the Spirit of Jesus Christ; that we—along with Christian believers of every race and nation—may truly be the body of Christ in the world, channeling his love to the community, especially to the hungry, the homeless, the sick, the prisoners, and all persons in need. Amen.

Waiting in a Doctor's Waiting Room

Kathy Halbrooks

LIVING CHRIST,

You were the Great Physician during the years of your earthly ministry. Persons with every kind of sickness or disability were drawn to you, and you responded with kindness and compassion. Your words and your touch restored their health, gave them a new lease on life, and filled their hearts with joy.

O Lord, you are the same loving, healing presence today as you were two thousand years ago. You are with all of us in this waiting room. Looking around, I see a lovely little girl—and I remember that you loved children and drew them to yourself. Heal this child, Jesus, and may her whole life be blessed by a personal awareness of your loving presence.

Around the room are several white-haired men and women, like myself. Those of us in older adulthood often need help in restoring our health and reducing our pain. Thank you for doctors, nurses, technicians, and office workers who form a healing team. Give them the insights, energy, and caring concern they need to help heal whole persons, not just physical bodies. Amen.

Waiting for Patience

Bruce Mosher

LOVING GOD,

Here we wait—wait for something to happen. Wait for others to make decisions—decisions that will affect our lives.

Help these individuals reach that decision. Give them understanding and trust in you.

Help us have patience—patience that, whatever the decision, it will be right with you and right for us too.

Give us also the understanding that yours is the glory.

Amen.

Waiting for Inner-City Schools to Improve

ALL-WISE HEAVENLY PARENT,

Jesus said that "the greatest and first commandment" is: "You shall love the Lord your God with all your heart, and with all your soul, and with *all your mind*" (Matt. 22:37-38, emphasis added). That love expresses our emotions; it also includes our full rational powers. You want us to think clearly about our relationship with you, O God, with our fellow human beings, and with the earth on which we live. That requires an excellent education, not a slipshod or incomplete approach to learning.

We feel real sadness, O God, when we read and hear that many inner-city schools have inadequate resources, such as books and laboratory equipment. Because of inadequate funds, inner-city schools frequently have less qualified teachers than suburban schools.

In the light of these facts, All-Wise Heavenly Parent, we feel an upsurge of hope as we learn about Teach for America. This program recruits top college graduates to attack educational inequities by teaching low-income students. Teach for America provides a fine focus for idealistic young adults who want to help all children and youth to gain an excellent education. Further, numerous political leaders are supporting Teach for America. For example, the mayor of Nashville, Tennessee, announced that fifty new college graduates in the TFA program will begin teaching in the city's inner-city schools.

Help all of us, O God, to think clearly as we seek effective answers to problems in our community. In this way we can show that we love you "with all our mind." Amen.

Waiting for the Computer to Boot and E-Mail to Come Up

Susan Ford Wiltshire

GOD WHO communicates,
even from a burning bush,

in the task
ahead I pray for

wisdom, to separate
the wheat from the chaff;

discernment, to pursue what is
important, not merely interesting;

and intuition, to spot some shyly hiding
human need where kindly words
    might help.

Amen.

Waiting for God's Healing Grace

Roela Victoria Rivera

LORD, I COME before your holy presence,
praying and waiting in deep silence.
You say, "Be still, and know that I am GOD";
"Trust in me with all your soul and heart."

Lord, I come with all my frailties,
surrendering my iniquities.
I sing, "Touch my body, touch my soul,
touch my spirit and make me complete."

I pray to you, God of all ages,
Source and fountain of healing grace.
I pray, Lord, heal my brokenness,
strengthen all my weaknesses.

God of mercy, Lord of love,
touch my being, my heart and soul.
Heal me, bless me, and make me whole.

A prayer from the heart for
your healing grace.

Waiting While Taking a Shower

JESUS CHRIST, Son of God, Savior,
Be in my eyes and in my seeing; in my ears
and in my hearing;
in my nose and in my breathing and in my
smelling;
in my mouth and in my speaking, singing,
praying, eating, kissing, and smiling.

Be in my hands and in my touching and
my working;
be in my feet and in my standing and in
my walking.
Be in my brain and in my thinking; in my
heart and in my feeling;
in my conscience and in my ethical decid-
ing; in my volition and in my willing;
in my fantasy and in my fantasizing,
so that nothing I do, say, think, feel—even
fantasize—shall separate me from you

but all shall enable me to know and to do
    your will this day.

O Christ, guide me; be on my left side and
    my right side
as the Companion of my way;
behind me to protect me; above me as my
    inspiration;
below me as my foundation; within me as
    the center of my being.

O God, by your grace enable me to grow
    into the fullness of the stature of Christ,
for I pray it in his name and for the sake of
    the world.
Amen.

Waiting for Jesus Christ to Be Raised from the Dead

GOD OF THE living and the dead,

Here we are on Holy Saturday, when our Lord Jesus Christ lay on a stone couch in a never-before-used tomb. Our hearts are filled with grief that Earth's most loving, most compassionate, most forgiving human being bore the brunt of beating, insults, mockery, and crucifixion—and still said in the midst of excruciating pain, "Father, forgive them; for they do not know what they are doing" (Luke 23:34).

It looked like utter failure for the grandest mission ever undertaken in the human family. Even today, the news is filled with accounts of massive killing in wars, horrible brutality against children—even by their parents; overwhelming greed and exploitation of the poor in many nations, including our own; and abusive treatment of Christians in some countries. How can we trust that you will triumph over so much evil? It often seems that we, like your Son Jesus, are sealed in a cold stone tomb!

O God, give us the grace to accept a time of death—of utter powerlessness—and trust you to raise us up to a new life of love, kindness, compassion, and nonviolence, in the constant company of our risen Lord Jesus Christ, for we pray it in his name and for the sake of the world. Amen.

Waiting for Power from God

O GOD, SOURCE of all life and power, we remember an instruction the risen Christ gave his disciples:

> Stay here in the city [Jerusalem]
> until you have been clothed with
> power from on high. (Luke 24:49)

As individuals and as a church, we are often impatient to overcome an injustice, such as racial or sexual discrimination, or to start a new program to meet an urgent human need, such as hunger, sickness, homelessness, or ignorance. But we know in our hearts that we desperately need power to do what you want. If you mean for us to do something great and world-transforming, you will give us the power to do it—but in your time. Help us to wait for it faithfully and expectantly.

Enable us to become a truly united body of Christ—through praying, thinking, and sharing—confident that you will use us to do your will in the world. May we be open to the Spirit's action through us in a new Pentecost. Amen.

Waiting for Christ to Come Again

ALL-POWERFUL AND mysterious God,

With Christians across many centuries we confidently proclaim:

Christ has died.

Christ is risen.

Christ will come again!

In today's world, so rife with wickedness, our hearts cry out: "When, O Lord? We need you now! Forces of evil seem to grow unchecked. Persons of goodwill slip toward the morass of despair. Only you, O God, know when the risen Christ will come to our fragile Earth."

We wait impatiently; give us the grace to wait, trusting that your time is always in time.

On days when we experience an upsurge of faith, we get glimpses of the risen Christ— in all loving deeds; in sharing of food, clothes, shelter, and medical care with the hungry and homeless; in visits with persons confined to hospitals and prisons; in witnesses of citizens speaking the truth to power in quest of justice for oppressed persons; in music, dances, and drama praising our Lord and Savior Jesus Christ.

Loving God, fill our hearts with joy and confidence that Christ will indeed come again. Amen.

Waiting for Jesus to Come Again

Frank E. Wier

ALMIGHTY GOD, Lord of the Universe,

Since I was converted a long time ago, I have been a pretty good boy (just kidding, okay?). I have been a regular churchgoer and student and have lived in an orderly way; I sing the hymns and pay attention to the prayers even more than the sermon.

At first, like when I was seventeen, Jesus seemed pretty close, but not any more. Religion has sustained me. Christianity has saved my life. No doubt about it. But I don't feel a burning heart. Shouldn't I? If Jesus is the center of everything that governs my life, shouldn't I feel his actual presence, as people claim to do?

I don't think what I felt as a young person was an illusion or just youthful exuberance. Help me get it back: "Come, Lord Jesus."

I wouldn't dare pray for a cosmic appearance, with the end of the world. I wouldn't want to ask you, Great and Merciful One, to cut off the future of every family and shut the doors on all potential future generations, just as things are starting to get really interesting.

But a *small* favor. Let Jesus come back into my life, where he once was, or where I thought he was; and then do the same for every Christian.

Revive us again; fill each heart with
    Thy love;
May each soul be rekindled with fire
    from above.*

    Amen.

*From hymn "Revive Us Again," by William P. Mackay (1837–1885)

Waiting for Tulips to Bloom

O GOD, CREATOR of all that is beautiful,
Here in Advent I loosen the soil,
planting bulbs a hand-span apart,
seeing in my mind's eye fields an ocean
    away
that exploded last spring in yellow, red,
    and white.

I marvel as I gouge out a six-inch grave
for each of these unimposing bulbs,
cover them with earth and pat each snugly
    in place.

Snow and rain and cold winds will blow.
Earth might seem inhospitable
to the quiet life within them;
but Spring will call them forth
To a riotous resurrection of colors.

I plant these bulbs as an act of faith:
O God, plant me too in your fertile earth
And prepare me for an Easter blooming!
    Amen.

Waiting for the Witness of the Holy Spirit

Bill Barnes

COME, HOLY SPIRIT,

Bear witness within me that I am a child of God, that we are children of God. Let your Spirit tell me who I am, who we are—not the voices of exploitation that constantly scream for my favor. Let that Identity Spirit mingle with my spirit and bring comfort and courage.

Come, Holy Spirit, bear witness within me that I—that we—are your children and heirs with Christ. Make me confident that your promises will really come off in fullness as I am faithful to your will. Grant me, by the gift of the Spirit, such hope and trust. Amen.

Waiting
for Change

Introduction
Quiet Time Before Social Action

AS A YOUNG MAN, I felt eager to get going quickly each morning, especially when I was working on a social program to remedy one of American society's glaring problems, such as racial or sex discrimination in employment, housing, or public accommodations. So a brief prayer before breakfast, a cursory survey of the newspaper, and I was off to the office or to a community meeting.

As an older adult, and especially in the post-retirement years, I have found it most productive to spend more time in prayer and reflection before I even glance at the newspaper—which all too often presents murder, rape, and mayhem (or misdoings of public officials) on the front page. I focus my mind and spirit on God's presence and call to discipleship before confronting the challenge of evil in my community and the larger world. This time of prayer and reflection arms me for conflict with evil and keeps me from being plunged into despair at the outset of a new day.

Across several years, I developed a prayer (with appropriate motions) that I pray each morning while taking a shower (see pages 110–11). Combining prayer with personal cleansing and the fact that the prayer is deeply rooted in my memory from thousands of repetitions make this private time a genuine experience of worship.

At breakfast, with a lighted candle on the table reminding me of Christ, the Light of the World, I thank God for the food and for the new day with all the opportunities it holds in store; and I lift up all my brothers and sisters who are hungry, with the hope that feeding programs may reach them and relieve their hunger.

After breakfast, I go to my reading chair in the living room for a time of devotions and prayer. I use the Bible, *The Upper Room* daily devotional guide, and some other printed materials; then I try to "be still and know that [God] is God." I lift up members of my family—immediate and extended; persons who are sick or undergoing surgery; hungry and homeless persons in my community and throughout our country; persons who are struggling with addictions; leaders of our community, state, and nation; members of the armed forces; prisoners; and then I pray for peace in the world—peace with justice—and name each country where I know there is war. I try to get quiet in mind and spirit and hear God speak to me, indicating what new or continued action God would have me do.

At this point I turn to the newspaper and read reflectively, finding places and causes that call me to add my voice (through telephone, U.S. mail, or e-mail) or action to help give hands and feet to my prayers.

Waiting for a Child to Be Born

CREATOR AND SUSTAINER of every human being,

As we wait nine months for our baby to be born, we are increasingly moved to awe as we participate in the miracle of birth. To think that one egg and one sperm cell can become a unique human being, a beautiful girl or a handsome boy with special talents and a unique personality, blows our minds!

As more and more family members and friends express their love and goodwill for this person-in-the-making, we become increasingly aware that our baby will be born into a loving community. May he or she respond to that circle of care in ways that will promote healthy growth and fulfillment of possibilities for a life of service and love in the world.

The world can be—and is, for all too many children—a frightening place. We see the birth of our child as an expression of faith in the future. Use our skills, talents, and wealth to make a better, nurturing world for our child and all of earth's children. We remember how Jesus loved children and what he told his followers:

> Let the little children come to me, and do not stop them; for it is to such as these that the kingdom of heaven belongs. (Matt. 19:14)

So we know that our baby's birth is not only a physical reality but the beginning of a spiritual journey to fellowship with the living Christ! Amen.

Waiting for Universal Health Care

LIVING CHRIST,

During your earthly ministry, you reached out to sick people wherever you went, and you healed them. We remember you not only as Teacher and Preacher but also as the Great Physician.

We are grateful for men and women who provide medical care, treating all our illnesses of mind and body. And we are thankful for health insurance that enables us to pay for that care.

But we are shocked to learn that more than forty-seven million people in the United States do not have health insurance. A major illness or hospitalization of a family member can bankrupt many of them. Fearing that outcome, some people may not seek needed medical care and thus become chronically ill or even die. That is a horrible—and unnecessary—situation in a nation as rich as the United States.

Sting our conscience, O God, and move us to provide health care for *all* citizens—children, women, and men—of every race, ethnic group, and economic level. In this way we can "do justice and love mercy" in our time. In this way, we can show that we love our neighbor as ourselves. Amen.

Waiting for Christmas to Arrive

HEAVENLY FATHER, who sent your Son Jesus Christ to us on the first Christmas,

As children we waited with barely restrained impatience for Christmas Day, which meant the excitement of new toys.

As adults we hastened to send out Christmas greetings to family and friends and waited with pleasant anticipation to see our children's joy as they opened each of their gifts.

As we have matured in faith, we experience Advent as a time for spiritual growth, for new insights into the meaning of Incarnation, and for deepening gratitude for your grace and generosity, O God, in sending Jesus Christ into the world.

Help us open our minds and hearts ever more fully to your love and to be channels of that love to an ever larger circle of family, friends, and persons in need. Amen.

Waiting for My Earthly Life to End

CREATOR AND SUSTAINER of all life,
Thank you for my body
with which for eighty-four years
I have been able to engage the universe.

For the loving circle of beings called
    "family"
I give you daily praise;
and for the expanded and expanding circle
of friends, dear as family,
I praise your generous grace.

For birds who swoop and swirl,
lifting my eyes heavenward,
I smile in pleasure.
For trees and flowers, I feel heartfelt delight;
For stars and planets, I am in awe.
For each new child, I overflow with joy and
    thanksgiving.

For our eternal Friend and brother, Jesus
    Christ,
I give you unending gratitude and praise.

And when my days are done,
Take me into your eternal chorus,
Where I may sing with joy in your universal
    family
And remember forever your gift of life on
    earth.
Amen.

Waiting for Divided Churches to Become One Body of Christ

GOD AND FATHER of Our Lord Jesus Christ,

We human beings have a tendency to splinter the human family into many groups, and—in sinful pride—to believe that our group is the right one, superior to all others. Even in the first century, humans demonstrated this characteristic, so the apostle Paul and other church leaders had to plead for unity and goodwill among Christians in the early church.

Unfortunately, across the twenty centuries until our own day, divisions among Christians have multiplied, and in many cases they have become deeper—and sometimes bitter. We know you do not intend such division for followers of your Son Jesus Christ. There have been, and are, honest efforts to heal these schisms, but we have a long way to go.

O God, we pray for wisdom, perseverance, and unflagging love as we pray for, work for, and witness for a truly united body of Christ throughout the whole world. We believe that as we wholeheartedly work for this united church, we shall see the face of the living Christ in the faces of our brothers and sisters who share that commitment. That will give us joy and staying power! Amen.

Waiting for the Abolition of the Death Penalty

O GOD, CREATOR and Sustainer of Life,

Ever since the days of Moses, we have heard your straightforward commandment: "You shall not murder" (Exod. 20:13). But many of us are reluctant to give up killing—both as individuals and as a society. Many states in the U.S. retain the death penalty, even though numerous innocent persons have been put to death. Our conscience is stung when we learn that ethnic minorities and poor people are executed in far greater numbers than affluent people.

Heavenly Father, make our hearts tender and compassionate toward all persons on death row. Strengthen our commitment to equal justice for all. Foster and sustain a our commitment to preserving life, and redirect the anger that prompts a desire to kill criminal offenders. Amen.

About the
Author-Editor

FRED CLOUD, A NATIVE of Arkansas, earned BA, MDiv, and DMin degrees at Vanderbilt University and an MA at Scarritt College. Ordained as a Methodist minister in 1946, he served pastorates in Tennessee for seven years; edited college-age magazines and books for the United Methodist Board of Education for fifteen years; and directed the Metro Human Relations Commission in Nashville, Tennessee, for twenty-three years.

As a sideline ministry, Fred taught in Vanderbilt Divinity School, Iliff School of Theology, Scarritt College, American Baptist College, and the University of Oklahoma. He assisted in developing Christian education materials in Europe, Southeast

Asia, and the South Pacific. He is the author of four books and numerous articles. His wife, Barbara Dickerson Cloud, served as a missionary in Japan before their marriage. Fred and Barbara live in Nashville and sing in the choir of Edgehill United Methodist Church.

Explore more prayer resources from Upper Room Books

Novena in a Time of War: Soul-Searching Prayers & Meditations by Jim Melchiorre

ISBN 978-0-8358-9940-6

"Must reading"—Tony Campolo

Talking in the Dark: Praying When Life Doesn't Make Sense by Steve Harper

ISBN 978-0-8358-9922-2

"A beam of light leading us to new depths of trust and surrender to the Holy One who hears our cries"—Susan Muto

A Life-Shaping Prayer: 52 Meditations in the Wesleyan Spirit by Paul Chilcote

ISBN 978-0-8358-9938-3

"A renewing journey into the presence of God"—Bishop Kenneth L. Carder

Creating a Life with God: The Call of Ancient Prayer Practices by Daniel Wolpert

ISBN 0-8358-9855-5

"An invitation to recognize and tend the longing of your heart"—Mark Yaconelli

Locked Up: Letters and Papers of a Prisoner of Conscience by Don Beisswenger

ISBN 978-0-8358-9939-0

"A strong and moving Christian witness"—Jane Vennard

To order
by phone~1.800.972.0433
online~www.UpperRoom.org/bookstore

or visit your local bookstore